The Death Of Food Deserts

30 Days Of Moving From Food
Deserts To Underground Food
Economies Using
Food Stamps

Taurian Deveaux

DEDICATION

This book is dedicated to the past, the present, and the future. To my ancestors and to all those who came before me who planted the way, to my dear friend Daveed who always encouraged my growth & to my daughter Meridian; good seed planted beside still waters.

PREFACE

This book is written from the premise of the first law of nature; Self-preservation. From such a fundamental starting place, it is imperative that every individual and community embrace access to sovereign, clean, healthy, and nutritious food irrespective of socioeconomic status, AS A HUMAN RIGHT.

I cannot tell you to break the law; however, I can tell you that any law that prevents the basic ethical survival of your family in accordance with food and nutrition is superseded by the higher law of self- preservation. Government has made it clear that they have no legal obligation to care for the citizen. You must commit to yourself, your family and your community, bringing forth intention coupled with consistent action. There is a way out of food deserts and into food surplus; a road to be carved out by our own hands.

Day 1:
Pool $300 in Food Stamps

For maximum effectiveness, $300 in Food Stamps is an excellent starting point. Of course, the more you have available to you as a group, the more you will be able to do. This is an ideal place from which to start, although many projects can be done on a 4 person family scale for as little as $100! Dollar amounts correlate with the times however you can always adjust these amounts as inflation rates change.

Create a list of potential contributors. Reach out to each and garner support for project. Listen to their feedback as well and document your progress below.

_____

_____

_____

_____

_____

_____

_____

_____

_____

_____

_____

_____

_____

_____

_____

_____

_____

_____

_____

_____

_____

_____

Day 2:
Include Families Using WIC

WIC participants receive an abundance of milk, breads, beans and other dry goods that they often have too much of. Extra milk can be converted into simple fresh cheese that lasts 3-5 days in the refrigerator.

Gather a list of people that would be interested in investing their excess supply into bigger food returns later. Find out exactly what they have in excess, how long they will receive it and plan from there.

Make a list of the items and start to brainstorm below ways to use them.

_____
_____
_____
_____
_____
_____
_____
_____
_____
_____
_____
_____
_____
_____
_____
_____
_____
_____
_____

Day 3:
Communicate Your Intentions

Be open with your participants about what you are doing and why. Illustrate for them the social justice and health disparities that go along with food deserts and how they impact all of our futures. Seek out elders and those who have experience as well as a can-do attitude.

Today, write down your plan of action in preparation of sharing. Then, write down your team and allies.

_____

_____

_____

_____

_____

_____

_____

_____

_____

_____

_____

_____

_____

_____

_____

_____

_____

_____

_____

_____

_____

_____

_____

_____

Day 4
Decide What Skills Need to Be Acquired

Learning curves can be steep. There are many skills you will need to learn to be successful. Use your time wisely. Don't waste time in experimental areas until you have the basics of traditional food preservation down.

Drying, pickling, salting, canning and fermentation are the foundation of extending the harvest. Give as much attention as possible to growing in these areas.

Today, try using YouTube as a resource for learning. Check out the wide variety of channels dedicated to such topics. Make a playlist for later viewing.

Find a recipe that calls for the implementation of one of the above techniques per item and build upon your skills.

What have you planned to learn?

_____

_____

_____

_____

_____

_____

_____

_____

_____

_____

_____

_____

_____

_____

_____

_____

_____

Day 5
Divide Labor Into Teams

Everything moves faster when everyone works as a team. Be like the ant. Each ant has its own job to do to ensure the progression of the nest. Gather your team and delegate. Divide labor based on experience and desire to learn. Every team should have one person who has committed to mastering an aspect of the operation and training those that join in.

Today, identify that key team member and together develop a handbook on procedure, process, and protocol for those that come after to follow.

_____
_____
_____
_____
_____
_____
_____
_____
_____
_____
_____
_____
_____
_____
_____
_____
_____
_____
_____
_____
_____
_____
_____
_____

Day 6
Use Simple Low Tech or No Tech Equipment

It's important to keep it simple and as cost effective as possible in the beginning. As you achieve greater levels of food security then you can invest in more equipment for streamlining operations. In the beginning, this is a guerrilla effort that must be powered by manpower when and where possible as well as advantageous.

Today, Research low tech but effective methods of gathering additional food supplies such as crab and shrimp farming being implemented in places like India and Africa or microgreens being grown for restaurants and homes throughout the USA.

What can you do to bring such efforts to your community?

_____
_____
_____
_____
_____
_____
_____
_____
_____
_____
_____
_____
_____
_____
_____
_____
_____
_____
_____

Day 7:
Plant What The Environment Supports

Don't waste time spinning your wheels. Time is of the essence, efficiency will be key in this process. The quickest way to move to food abundance is to plant food that is naturally supported by your environment and season.

There are plenty of resources online and in your local library that can teach you about different produce and growing techniques for your climate.

Research your zone and microclimate and make a list of what can be suitable to grow in your area. Be sure to chart out which months are best for planting and harvesting, as well as what plants complement each other. For example, some plants provide natural pest control while others may fix nitrogen in the soil.

_____

_____

_____

_____

_____

_____

_____

_____

_____

_____

_____

_____

_____

_____

_____

_____

_____

_____

_____

_____

Day 8:
Make Value Added Products Top Priority

Put the group's expertise and newly acquired skills in drying, pickling, salting, canning and fermentation to use by creating "Value Added Products".

These are food items that have been altered from their original state to increase their value to the consumer. Examples of Value Added Products are strawberry jam, beef jerky, pickled eggs, and relish.

Write down five value added products based on your groups desires and find resources on how to produce them. Devise a plan to implement the production of the products in alignment with harvest time.

_____

_____

_____

_____

_____

_____

_____

_____

_____

_____

_____

_____

_____

_____

_____

_____

_____

_____

_____

_____

Day 9:
Save Seeds

Seed saving, seed swapping, and heirlooms are the building blocks of reversing food deserts. The more a community controls their own food, it's distribution, accessibility and variety, the better health outcomes will be.

Heirloom fruits and vegetables outperform their conventional counterparts in yield, flavor, and nutritional value.

Explore free seed catalogs and websites. Read descriptions of what originates from your region and what grows native to the region as well. Make efforts to grow and save these seeds over the seasons. Eventually you will not have to purchase any new seed if you save them well.

Today, find at least five opportunities to gather seeds free of charge. Delegate the task of acquiring seed and starting a seed library to a team member.

_____

_____

_____

_____

_____

_____

_____

_____

_____

_____

_____

_____

_____

_____

_____

_____

_____

Day 10:
Make Friends with Local Farmers

Get to know who is growing what in your area. Find out if any are able to accept Food Stamps directly. A good place to start your search may be a Farmers Market. All counties have Farmers Markets that can accept Food Stamps and some may even match you dollar for dollar.

Relationships are important. Spend time getting to know the farmers and their needs. Talk to the local farmers and explain to them what you are in the process of doing and your goals. They may be able to assist with bulk items at a great rate or even be able to provide knowledge and assistance.

Today, find 4 opportunities to visit a farmer's market in the next month. Put them on your calendar. If you can find out which farms will be in attendance, reach out to them prior to the event.

_____
_____
_____
_____
_____
_____
_____
_____
_____
_____
_____
_____
_____
_____
_____
_____
_____

Day 11:
Bring Back Community Specific Traditional Services

Remember Meat Men, Milk Men & Cart Vendors?
Patronage of local traditional food vendors helps to keep things fresh. Shopping regionally reduces food mileage, thereby reducing its cost.

These informal distribution channels also help sure-up communities in times of crisis. Take time to map out the informal food channels in your community and develop open lines of communication.

Put together an action plan that helps both parties reach their goals. One example of this would be striking up a deal with the local small dairy farmer who recently lost their contract to sell a portion of their milk to your collective.

_____
_____
_____
_____
_____
_____
_____
_____
_____
_____
_____
_____
_____
_____
_____
_____
_____

Day 12:
Reward Recycling and Returns

Reduction of waste is a key part of reversing food deserts and should be emphasized.

Reward recycling and returns by offering discounts. For example, a fruit cart vendor may agree to give $0.05 off per bag to each customer who provide their own bags. It helps the consumer save as well as the vendor, all while doing one's part to reduce the use of plastic

What are a few incentives you can provide to encourage waste reduction?

_____
_____
_____
_____
_____
_____
_____
_____
_____
_____
_____
_____
_____
_____
_____
_____
_____
_____
_____
_____
_____
_____

Day 13:
Upcycle Fabric to Create Grocery Sacks & Wax Cloth

Thread important principles such as zero waste into the program by upcycling fabrics to create sacks and wax cloths.

These can be cheaply made in beautiful colors and patterns, reducing plastics as well as providing an additional revenue stream for the program.

There may be persons in your collective who have a gift for upcycling. Today, take the time to ask if anyone would like to lead this particular effort. Research online for a few starter ideas you may be able to implement immediately.

What can you plan to do in the near future?

_____
_____
_____
_____
_____
_____
_____
_____
_____
_____
_____
_____
_____
_____
_____
_____
_____
_____
_____
_____
_____

Day 14:
Save Scraps for Livestock

Reduction of feed cost is always a priority for anyone raising livestock. Food scraps also provide much welcomed variety for the animals.

Getting the entire group to pitch in by saving kitchen scraps can add up to hundreds of dollars saved over an operation's lifetime. Ask the community to save their scraps and be diligent about collection.

Create a schedule for collecting the scraps. Additionally plan how you will store and disperse the collection.

_____
_____
_____
_____
_____
_____
_____
_____
_____
_____
_____
_____
_____
_____
_____
_____
_____
_____
_____
_____
_____
_____

Day 15:
Make it as Aesthetically Appealing As Possible

People love sizzle more than steak so give them sizzle along with your solid offering. It has to catch the eye. Make it look stellar and people will naturally be drawn to support what you are doing.

This is the age of photo ops and experience driven living. Take pictures that entice and make your audience want to be a part of what you are doing.

Today, begin to recognize photo opportunities to tell a story for your initiative. Research what popular brands do to visually appeal and borrow from their techniques. Write out possible upcoming opportunities.

_____

_____

_____

_____

_____

_____

_____

_____

_____

_____

_____

_____

_____

_____

_____

_____

_____

_____

_____

_____

_____

_____

Day 16:
Be Ready To Explain

As word grows, you will get people who may not understand how such a system works as well as your product offerings. Be open to questions and be able to answer them concisely.

Today, to help communicate your group's ethos to new members and potential clients create an FAQ (Frequently Asked Questions) document for them.

_____

_____
_____
_____
_____
_____
_____
_____
_____
_____
_____
_____
_____
_____
_____
_____
_____
_____
_____
_____
_____
_____
_____
_____

Day 17:
Produce According To Thrift Harvest

Make all ingredients count. Research recipes from hard time eras such as the Great Depression and World War 2. These recipes are perfect for reversing food deserts as they contain only a few ingredients that can be commonly found at an affordable price in both urban and rural communities. They also employ the use of ingredients that are versatile enough to make a variety of products.

Today, gather recipes that will serve you well by researching old cookbooks from times of lack. This will be a good starting point.

What have you learned by reading?

_____

_____

_____

_____

_____

_____

_____

_____

_____

_____

_____

_____

_____

_____

_____

_____

_____

_____

_____

_____

Day 18:
Focus On Fast Producing Livestock

Your key objective for this project should be moving towards
sovereign and self-sufficient food security systems. One of the
vital ways to achieve such a goal and produce food of good
nutritional value that is both sovereign and self-sufficient is to
include livestock.

In cases of emergency, you need to have food that produces fast
and moves with you. Consider raising rabbits as every group
member can assist with a small space. They have a short 30-day
gestation cycle resulting in numerous rabbits, which can be
raised out for meat.

Today, research what may be the best livestock to begin raising
using the current resources you have. Take inventory of those
willing to help raise them. Map out a plan to prepare to acquire
the animals.

_____

_____

_____

_____

_____

_____

_____

_____

_____

_____

_____

_____

_____

_____

_____

_____

_____

_____

_____

Day 19:
Make Use of Free Seeds, Trees and Scions

Seeds, scions, trees and other planting materials can often be acquired free of charge via your local County Extension Office as well as local colleges and universities within your state.

Check online databases to see what is available as they are updated regularly. Heirloom seed companies are on the front line of education and access as well, with some regularly distributing free seed to underserved communities throughout the year.

Use the list you created earlier and begin to collect seeds. Today, schedule with your suppliers times to pick up seeds or arrange for them to be shipped to you.

_____
_____
_____
_____
_____
_____
_____
_____
_____
_____
_____
_____
_____
_____
_____
_____
_____
_____
_____
_____

Day 20:
Buy and Make Use of Produce That Can Be Used In Variety of Money Making Ways.

When planning what to produce always think around the concept of a market garden. What can be useful for my family and others as well? What crops can I plant or livestock can I produce that will serve me in a multiplicity of ways?

For example, a crop of heirloom tomatoes can be sold fresh, sun dried, turned into a sauce, canned and the seeds can be dried and sold or stored for later use. A goat will provide milk, meat, offspring, and pelleted manure.

Today, use the knowledge you gained learning about what to plant in your area, to map out a plan for a garden.

_____
_____
_____
_____
_____
_____
_____
_____
_____
_____
_____
_____
_____
_____
_____
_____
_____
_____
_____
_____
_____

Day 21:
Incorporate Permaculture Principles

Permaculture principles are simply a return to the way humans have intersected with their natural environment for thousands of years. It fosters symbiotic relationships, promotes diversity, and produces no waste.

Permaculture principles can be incorporated in both the division of labor with everyone contributing to the food ecosystem as well as in the actual things being produced, I.e. offering diverse products and a focus on thrift-harvest.

After researching ways you can create a symbiotic relationship with nature, create three processes that will benefit both you and the environment. Share them with your team and create ways to enforce the proper implementation.

_____
_____
_____
_____
_____
_____
_____
_____
_____
_____
_____
_____
_____
_____
_____
_____
_____
_____
_____

Day 22:
Employ Youth As Errand Runners

Bringing the next generation fully into the fold is essential to the death of food deserts. Not only do they need to know how to produce, they also need to learn the business side of production as well as network with those who make use of the things produced.

Making deliveries, taking orders and other work that does not need expertise are ideal ways to start familiarizing youth with the system, helping them grow their confidence and observe a number of roles, eventually finding their rightful place in the food justice movement.

You can create flyers, approach church groups, the YMCA, Boys & Girls Clubs and other like-minded youth focused groups. Inform them about what you are doing and see if they would like to be involved. Offer youth local to the community employment first and then expand from there.

What are a few ways you may be able to utilize youth participation?

_____
_____
_____
_____
_____
_____
_____
_____
_____
_____
_____
_____
_____
_____

Day 23:
Stay On Top of Health & Safety with Checklists, Checks and Balances, Monitoring

It's your personal responsibility to yourself and the communities you serve to run a clean and ethical operation. Be honest with your consumers about the fact that this is a guerilla effort to pull oneself up by the bootstraps.

Even if you cannot afford certain certifications, make it a point to learn all the same information and put it into practice as best as you can.

Don't be afraid to ask for help from those who have been at this longer than you. Go online and look up the department that handles the safety factors for your area of choice. Review their regulations and take advantage of the free courses and webinars offered through their office and website.

Today, find at least three in person classes or workshops and put them on your calendar.

Write out the information you need to gather and learn.

_____
_____
_____
_____
_____
_____
_____
_____
_____
_____
_____
_____
_____
_____

Day 24:
Secure Distribution Channels

Securing distribution channels are on par with self- sufficient production in terms of importance.

Without secure distribution channels, milk gets produced but must be dumped, strawberries are harvested that never make it to one's plate and eggs pile up and spoil, discouraging producers and eating entire profit margins.

Do not wait for big overarching distribution; do employ guerilla tactics and organize distribution around traditional factions of neighborhood meat men, fruit carts, and rolling markets. The more people involved in the distribution of food the more variety of food we will be able to secure now as well as in times of crisis.

Today, gather your team and create a plan for distribution. Be sure to create a document for others to refer to as needed.

_____
_____
_____
_____
_____
_____
_____
_____
_____
_____
_____
_____
_____
_____
_____
_____
_____
_____

Day 25:
Start Your Own Farmers Market

Farmer's Markets are the perfect place to showcase the best and brightest of what you have to offer. There is a Farmer's Market every day of the week in most major U.S. cities and communities are starting new ones every day.

It's an ideal place to foster a culture of self-sufficiency, resilience and offer immediate response to the needs of the people. It's also a fantastic incubator space for both producers and buyers as every farmer's market currently accepts Food Stamps.

Ask the community you serve what their major pain points are around the issue of food and customize your Farmers Market to address those needs.

Take the time to delegate certain tasks to your team, such as marketing, soliciting vendors, acquiring space and collecting the proper permits.

_____
_____
_____
_____
_____
_____
_____
_____
_____
_____
_____
_____
_____
_____
_____
_____
_____
_____

Day 26:
Start Your Own Street Food Market

Street Food Markets vary from traditional Farmers Markets in the fact that they focus on hot and cold ready-made meals to be consumed right there or packed and enjoyed at home later.

This is a sector in which disenfranchised communities have thrived and continue to thrive. Take full advantage of cultural food phenomena and people's natural curiosity to promote your products to a wider audience.

Street markets always draw in tourism, which equals more financial stability and expanded opportunities for growth.

Like the Farmer's Market, take the time to plan the entire event from start to finish with your team. Today, make the itinerary for an organized meeting to get the job done.

_____
_____
_____
_____
_____
_____
_____
_____
_____
_____
_____
_____
_____
_____
_____
_____
_____
_____
_____

Day 27:
Use Food Stamps to Purchase Organic Beans, Grains, Garlic
& Legumes from Bulk Bins for Planting

Both local Mom & Pops as well as major food chains offer a variety of seeds and bulbs that can be direct planted for an abundant harvest. This is an affordable way to start on the road to both self-sufficiency and surpluses. Seeds acquired in this fashion are perfect for a market garden, as they have already been proven popular with both consumers and suppliers.

Take a trip to your local grocery and explore the varieties available. Select seed stock and plant according to your season, zone, and microclimate. Use the information you have gathered prior to assist in your selection.

Once your garden has been mapped out, begin sorting and storing your seeds.

_____
_____
_____
_____
_____
_____
_____
_____
_____
_____
_____
_____
_____
_____
_____
_____
_____
_____

Day 28:
Start A Homestead Sized Goat Dairy with $150

Goat's milk is a nutritious addition to any community suffering from food insecurity. Goat's milk is more easily digested; they are easy to keep, clean and can give you a sizeable amount of milk for a family of four. Goat's milk can also be turned into delicious cheese and gentle soaps. Excess can be traded with friends and neighbors.

Read up on what a quality goat looks like and take a trip to a livestock auction. If you do not know where to find one, look online, you may be surprised at how close one may be. You can likely find a pregnant Nigerian Dwarf for a great price. Once she is in good stride, she can be milked once or twice daily. Nigerian Dwarfs are renowned for producing excellent quality milk with a higher butterfat content at the nearly the same production rate of a full sized doe.

Today, find resources that may help you in learning to house and raise a goat, as well as ways to use the resources it will provide. Write out what you find.

_____
_____
_____
_____
_____
_____
_____
_____
_____
_____
_____
_____
_____
_____

Day 29:
Keep Production Pipelines Full

Reversing food desertification has as much to do with creating variety, fostering traditional food cultures and putting production back in the hands of the people as it has to do with accessibility, control, and distribution. Global food culture presents hundreds of springboards that can create micro food economies for the communities that embrace them.

In the city of Los Angeles alone, each roadside BBQ, elote cart, cake lady doing her rounds in the cities barber and beauty shops, fresh handmade tortilla and beans served with hot chocolate in the early hours of the morning, represent the underground food economy that is driven by ethnogeographic tastes. These should be encouraged and those engaged should be consistently investing in ways to expand the business and the variety of goods they create.

Look at your community's food heritage for inspiration and write a list of all the foods that are unique and special or popular. Determine if any can be made commercially viable and provide an important addition for the community you serve.

_____
_____
_____
_____
_____
_____
_____
_____
_____
_____
_____
_____
_____
_____

Day 30:
Document Your Progress

Documentation is important not only as data collection but to chart progress, assess emergency situations quicker and create transferable models that can be implemented in a variety of community spaces. As the saying goes, "If you didn't write it down it didn't happen". Record keeping is for you and your key stakeholders in the program however, it serves as an essential aid if you ever have to use them for official purposes.

Today, create a system of ledgers to track your progress. Additionally, develop metrics and evaluation tools to judge your progress

Keep up the same energy you have had throughout this journey to continue your efforts.

_____
_____
_____
_____
_____
_____
_____
_____
_____
_____
_____
_____
_____
_____
_____
_____
_____
_____

ABOUT THE AUTHOR

Taurian Deveaux is the founding director of Taurian Deveaux's Agronomy & Music Ministry, a nonprofit that focuses on music programs, outreach, and teaching sustainable living through agriculture to people in urban and rural communities.

Taurian got her start early in the back gardens of her great-grandmother's yards and carried her passion for the natural world onto the U.K where she learned all about allotment gardens, home economics and the defined role each individual has in what they eat. As an adult, she spent many years traveling to places throughout the world to learn about our collective food heritage as well as witness how agriculture intersects with everyday life. She currently farms and teaches in Southern California.